A
in the Sky

Kate Scott

OXFORD
UNIVERSITY PRESS

OXFORD
UNIVERSITY PRESS

Great Clarendon Street, Oxford, OX2 6DP, United Kingdom

Oxford University Press is a department of the University of Oxford. It furthers the University's objective of excellence in research, scholarship, and education by publishing worldwide. Oxford is a registered trade mark of Oxford University Press in the UK and in certain other countries

Text © Kate Scott 2014

The moral rights of the author have been asserted

First published 2014

All rights reserved. No part of this publication may be reproduced, stored in a retrieval system, or transmitted, in any form or by any means, without the prior permission in writing of Oxford University Press, or as expressly permitted by law, by licence or under terms agreed with the appropriate reprographics rights organization. Enquiries concerning reproduction outside the scope of the above should be sent to the Rights Department, Oxford University Press, at the address above.

You must not circulate this work in any other form and you must impose this same condition on any acquirer

British Library Cataloguing in Publication Data
Data available

ISBN: 978-0-19-830822-5

10 9 8 7 6 5 4 3

Paper used in the production of this book is a natural, recyclable product made from wood grown in sustainable forests. The manufacturing process conforms to the environmental regulations of the country of origin.

Printed in China by Leo Paper Products Ltd

Acknowledgements

Series Editor: Nikki Gamble
Illustrated by Natalie Hughes
Cover photos: Arc-Pic.com; Maksym Darakchi/Shutterstock; Serg Zastavkin/Shutterstock

The publisher would like to thank the following for permission to reproduce photographs: **p1**: AndreAnita/Shutterstock; **p2-3**: Corbis/Mary Ann McDonald; **p4-5**: Naturepl.com/Andy Sands; **p6**: www.arc-pic.com; **p7**: Graham Eaton/Nature Picture Library; **p9**: Mark Carwardine/Nature Picture Library; **p10-11**: Alamy/WorldFoto; **p12**: Getty Images/Aurelie and Morgan David de Lossy; **p13**: Mark Carwardine/Nature Picture Library; **p14**: Jakub Mrocek/Shutterstock; **p15t**: Bousfield/iStockphoto; **p15b**: www.arc-pic.com; **p16**: naturepl.com/Peter Lewis; **p17**: Roger Hall/Shutterstock; **p18**: ArcticPhoto/T.Jacobsen; **p19**: Alamy/BCS; **p20-21**: www.arc-pic.com; **p22-23**: www.arc-pic.com; **p24**: David Tipling/Nature Picture Library

Contents

A Life in the Sky	4
Waiting	6
Taking Flight	8
Plunge Dive and Surface Dip	10
A Sea Swallow	12
Finding a Mate	14
First Flight	16
Defending the Family	18
To the Sky Again	20
Around the World and Back Again	22
Glossary and Index	24

A Life in the Sky

I am an Arctic tern — I live in the air.
My home is up in the wide, wide sky.
I fly past cloud after cloud after cloud ...

The Arctic tern spends almost its whole life flying — it can even eat and sleep while it flies! During its life, the Arctic tern flies three times as far as the moon and back.

That's 2.4 million kilometres (km) — 1.5 million miles!

The Arctic tern's journey

When the tern goes to the **Arctic**, it flies over the middle of the Atlantic Ocean.

↑ to the Arctic

This small bird only weighs as much as a cup of sugar (around 100 to 115 grams). But it can fly for 17 700 km (11 000 miles) at a time!

the Arctic

Greenland

Atlantic Ocean

Africa

South America

Antarctica

When the tern goes to **Antarctica**, it either flies along the African coast or follows the South American coast.

↓ to Antarctica

Waiting

*I watch and I wait while my feathers fall.
I wait to soar into that wide, wide sky.*

In December, January and February, the Arctic tern rests on the sea ice in Antarctica. While it is there, it **moults** its wing feathers. The Arctic tern sometimes loses its feathers so quickly that it can't fly at all for a little while!

Antarctica contains 90 per cent of the world's ice, but because it hardly ever rains here, it can be called a desert!

the Arctic

Antarctica

The Arctic tern spends much of its life flying between the Arctic and Antarctica.

It is very difficult for wildlife to survive in the middle of Antarctica because it is so cold and dry. This is why the animals of Antarctica live in the ocean or by the coast.

Some fish in Antarctica have a special antifreeze chemical in their blood which stops them from freezing, but it doesn't protect them from the Arctic tern!

Antarctica

Taking Flight

The wind lifts my wings.
I trace the edge of land and sea,
then cross the ocean to another coast.
I am skimming the sky.

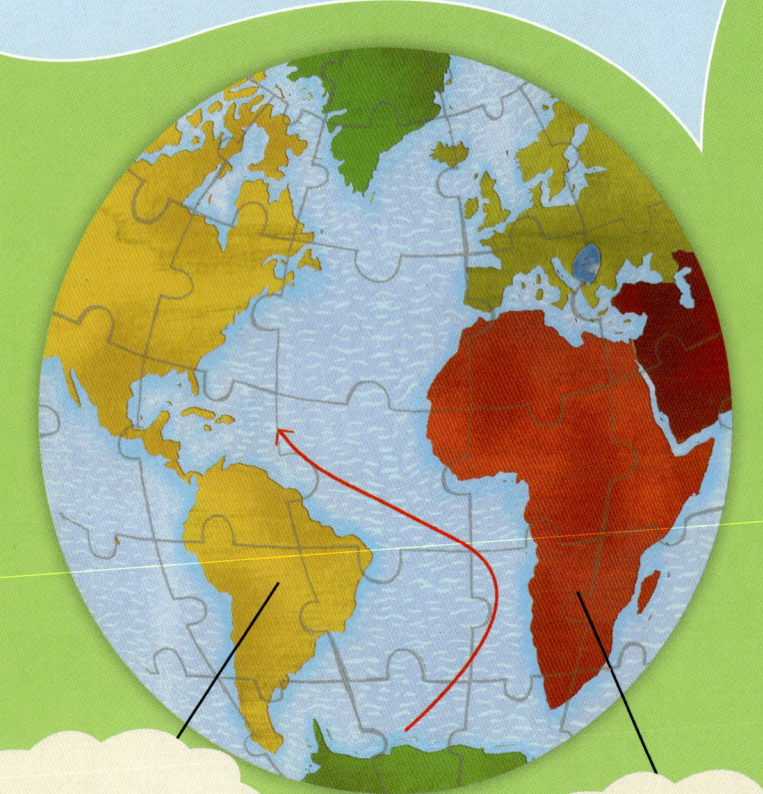

Southern Africa

South America

South America

Southern Africa

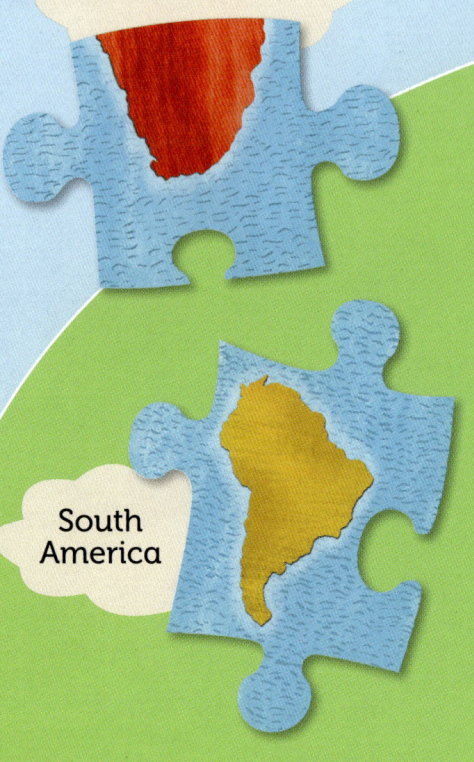

The Arctic tern leaves Antarctica and flies north towards the Arctic. It doesn't fly in a straight line, though! First it follows the coast of Southern Africa. Then it flies across the Atlantic Ocean to the coast of South America.

No one is sure why the birds take this **zigzagging** route. It might be so that they don't have to fly into the wind – which makes flying much harder work!

When the Arctic tern is flying north, it travels about 520 km (323 miles) per day. It would take about two weeks for most people to walk that far – or even longer!

Plunge Dive and Surface Dip

I dive through air to dip in the waves.
I'm quick and sharp and bold — I grab my fish!

When they need food, Arctic terns **hover** over the water, then zoom down to grab fish or shrimp from the surface of the water. They sometimes eat insects as they fly.

plunge diving

surface dipping

Arctic terns usually only dive 50 cm underneath the waves.

Sometimes Arctic terns steal fish from other birds. They do this by flying towards them very fast. The other bird is surprised and drops its fish!

The Arctic tern stops over the Atlantic Ocean to catch fish. The tern needs lots of energy to fly such a long way!

Atlantic Ocean

A Sea Swallow

Soon I will reach the other side of the world.
I will find a family of my own.
My own flock to fly with across the wide sky.

the Arctic

By the time the Arctic tern reaches the Arctic, it will have flown 25 700 km (15 969 miles). It will have been almost constantly in the air for 40 days!

The Arctic tern is often called the 'sea swallow'. Like the swallow, it has long, slender wings and long tail feathers. The tern's wings are about 80 cm across.

Finding a Mate

*I see her and show her how I fly.
I soar, I swoop, I chase.*

The Arctic tern arrives in Greenland, where the terns gather to **mate**. Most Arctic terns mate for life. They may be together for as long as 30 years.

Arctic terns attract a mate by showing off their flying skills. Then the male catches a fish and offers it to the female.

Greenland

The terns find a place to have their eggs. The female lays her eggs in a shallow hole in the ground called a scrape.

The birds line the scrape with shells, grass or little stones. It takes around 24 days for the eggs to **hatch**.

15

First Flight

I feed my children to make them strong.
They grow and grow.
One day they stretch their wings.
I show them how to lift on the wind,
how to fly to the clouds.

Once the eggs have hatched, the parents feed their babies until they are old enough to fly and feed themselves. With such a long journey in front of them, these baby birds need to grow strong!

Defending the Family

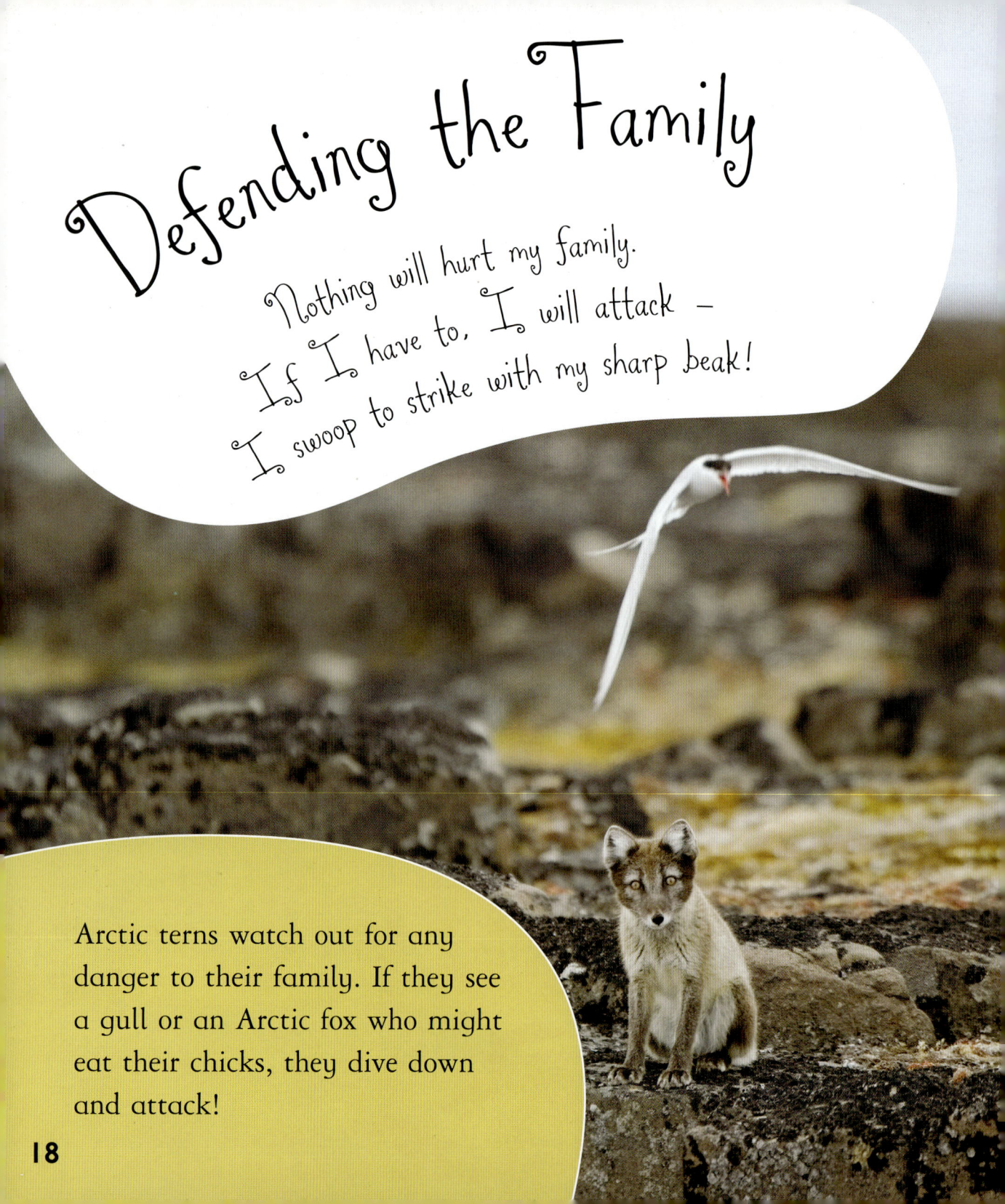

Nothing will hurt my family.
If I have to, I will attack —
I swoop to strike with my sharp beak!

Arctic terns watch out for any danger to their family. If they see a gull or an Arctic fox who might eat their chicks, they dive down and attack!

People trying to watch or photograph Arctic terns have also been landed on and pecked – hard!

To the Sky Again

It is time to leave, time to take to the sky.

But now I am not alone.

We will soar together.

We will fly to find another summer.

When the Arctic tern and its family are ready to fly, they set off with a **colony** of terns and fly all the way back to Antarctica.

Antarctica

A few years ago, tiny **tracking devices** were attached to some Arctic terns. They proved that the Arctic tern flies further than any other **migrating** bird!

Around the World and Back Again

*I am a bird of flight.
My home is up in the wide, wide sky.
I fly past cloud after cloud after cloud ...*

The Arctic tern probably spends more time in daylight than any other animal. When the days get shorter in Antarctica, it leaves and heads north.

When the days get shorter in the Arctic, it heads south. Maybe it loves the daylight and that is why it spends so much time in the air.

The Arctic tern travels further than any other bird in the world. Its life is one amazing journey!

23

Glossary

Antarctica: the area near the South Pole

Arctic: the area near the North Pole

colony: a group of animals

hatch: to come out of an egg

hover: to stay in the same place in the air

mate: to have babies / a partner to have babies with

migrating: travelling to a different place

moults: loses old feathers once a year so new ones can grow

tracking devices: machines or tools that follow the movements of something or someone

zigzagging: twisting, not straight

Index

Antarctica	5, 6, 7, 8, 21, 22
Arctic	5, 7, 8, 12, 22
dive	10, 11, 18
eggs	15, 17
feathers	6, 13
fish	7, 10, 11, 14
mate	14
wings	8, 13, 16